# Doggie Data

# Labrador Retrievers

## ELIZABETH NOLL

BLACK
RABBIT
BOOKS

Bolt is published by Black Rabbit Books
P.O. Box 3263, Mankato, Minnesota, 56002.
www.blackrabbitbooks.com
Copyright © 2018 Black Rabbit Books

Jennifer Besel, editor; Grant Gould, interior
designer; Michael Sellner, cover designer;
Omay Ayres, photo researcher

Library of Congress Cataloging-in-Publication Data
Names: Noll, Elizabeth, author.
Title: Labrador retrievers / by Elizabeth Noll.
Description: Mankato, Minnesota : Black Rabbit Books, [2018] | Series:
Bolt. Doggie data | Audience: Ages 9-12. | Audience: Grades 4 to 6. |
Includes bibliographical references and index.
Identifiers: LCCN 2016049957 (print) | LCCN 2017003483 (ebook) | ISBN
9781680721539 (library binding) | ISBN 9781680722178 (e-book) | ISBN
9781680724561 (paperback)
Subjects: LCSH: Labrador retriever–Juvenile literature.
Classification: LCC SF429.L3 N65 2018 (print) | LCC SF429.L3 (ebook) |
DDC 636.752/7-dc23
LC record available at https://lccn.loc.gov/2016049957

Printed in the United States at CG Book Printers,
North Mankato, Minnesota, 56003. 3/17

# Contents

# CHAPTER 1

# Meet the

# Labrador Retriever

The Labrador retriever races through the park. It skids to a stop when it reaches the stick its owner threw. The dog picks the stick up and returns it to its owner. The playful dog waits for another throw. Then it sets off again. This dog loves to play and make its owner happy.

# Lean on Me

Labrador retrievers are smart, patient, and gentle dogs. They make good pets for families with children. Many Labs are also trained to be service dogs. These dogs help blind or **disabled** people.

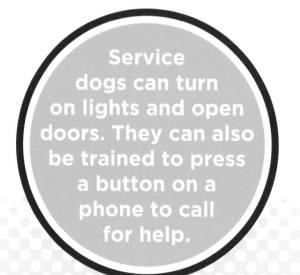

Service dogs can turn on lights and open doors. They can also be trained to press a button on a phone to call for help.

**WATER-RESISTANT COAT**

**MUSCULAR TAIL**

**WIDE HEAD**

**KIND EYES**

**WEBBED PAWS**

9

## TOP 10 MOST POPULAR
Dogs in the United States in 2015

| 1 | 2 | 3 | 4 |
|---|---|---|---|
| Labrador Retrievers | German Shepherds | Golden Retrievers | Bulldogs |

# CHAPTER 2

# A Special Personality

Labs are known for being friendly. They are also kind and **loyal**. They want to help their owners. Labs are the most popular type of dog in the United States.

| 5 | 6 | 7 | 8 | 9 | 10 |
|---|---|---|---|---|---|
| Beagles | French Bulldogs | Yorkshire Terriers | Poodles | Rottweilers | Boxers |

# Go Fetch!

Labs are good pets for children. They are playful and friendly. They also have lots of energy. These dogs love to run and play with kids. Kids often tire of playing fetch before their dogs.

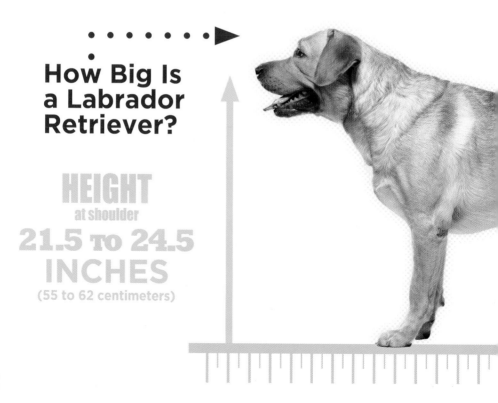

## How Big Is a Labrador Retriever?

**HEIGHT**
at shoulder
**21.5 TO 24.5 INCHES**
(55 to 62 centimeters)

40 50

30

20

80

10

90

0

100

pounds

pounds

**WEIGHT**
**55 to 80**
**POUNDS**
(25 to 36 kilograms)

Brown Labs are called "chocolate" Labs. But yellow Labs aren't called "lemon."

# CHAPTER 3

# Labrador Retrievers'

# Features

Labs are medium-sized dogs. They weigh up to 80 pounds (36 kg).

They have short hair. Their coats come in three colors. They can be black, yellow, or chocolate.

## Super Swimmer

Labs are strong and fast. They are very good swimmers. They have webs between their toes. The webs help them swim. Their long toes help them swim too.

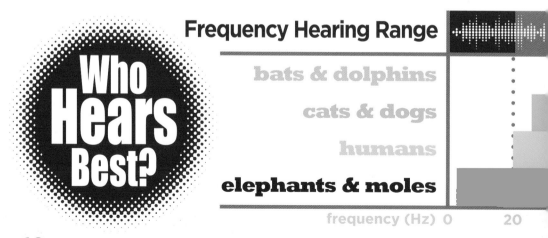

**Frequency Hearing Range**

bats & dolphins

cats & dogs

humans

**elephants & moles**

frequency (Hz) 0          20

Who Hears Best?

20,000     40,000         160,000

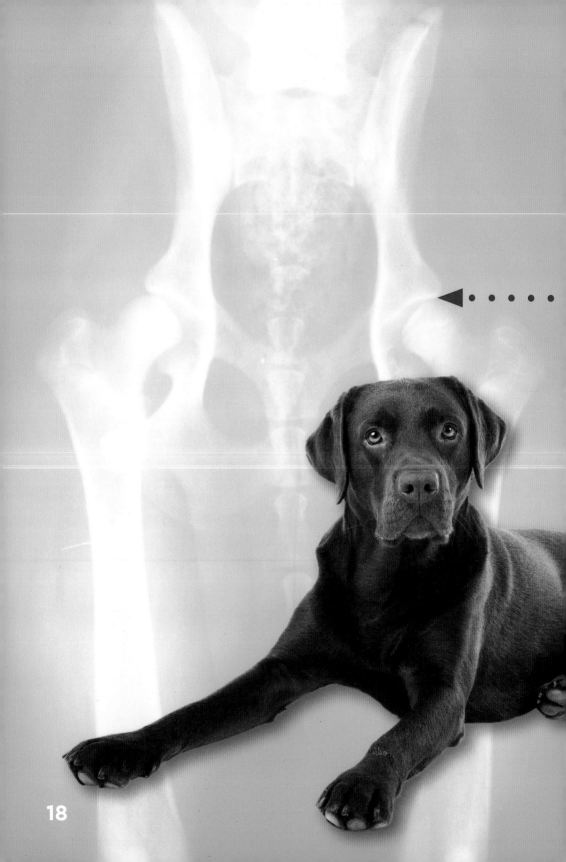

# Health Problems

As Labs grow older, they often have pain in their hips. Their bones don't fit together correctly. This disease is called hip **dysplasia**.

## Number of Dogs with Dysplasia in One Study

total dogs studied: 248,657

**12.2%** had dysplasia

# Labrador Retriever Life Cycle

Newborn Labs weigh about 1 pound (.5 kg).

**PUPPY**

Labs become seniors when they're seven to 10 years old.

ADOLESCENT

Young Labs might not follow rules they followed as puppies.

ADULT

Labs are fully grown in about 18 months.

SENIOR

# CHAPTER 4

#  Caring

# for Labrador Retrievers

All dogs need regular vet checkups. They also need care at home. Labs need lots of exercise. A 10-minute walk won't be enough. They need at least an hour of exercise each day.

• • • • • • • • • • • • • • • • • • • • • •

Dogs stick their heads out of car windows for the smells.

# What Labs Need

food and water

exercise

company

# Run, Drink, Eat, Play

Labs need food and water, of course. They also need baths when they get dirty. Some experts suggest weekly brushing. Others say there's no need.

Another thing Labs want is company. These dogs will chew anything if left alone too long.

## Loyal and Loving

Labs are loyal and loving dogs. They do need plenty of attention. They can also need special medical care. But owners say their pups are worth it.

# Is a Labrador Retriever

## Right for You?

Answer the questions below. Then add up your points to see if a Lab is a good fit.

**1** **What's your favorite thing to do outside?**

A. Sit and read. **(1 point)**

B. Play a game with friends. **(2 points)**

C. Throw a slobbery ball over and over. **(3 points)**

28

## 2 How do you feel about doggy kisses?

A. Yuck! **(1 point)**

B. They're OK once in awhile. **(2 points)**

C. They're the best! **(3 points)**

## 3 What kind of coat do you like?

A. soft and thick **(1 point)**

B. curly and messy **(2 points)**

C. smooth and sleek **(3 points)**

{
**3 points**
**A Lab is not your best match.**
**4–8 points**
**You like Labs, but another breed might be better for you.**
**9 points**
**A Lab would be a great buddy for your life!**
}

**adolescent** (ad-oh-LES-uhnt)—a young person or animal that is developing into an adult

**disabled** (dys-A-buhld)—unable to perform one or more activities because of illness, injury, or other problems

**dysplasia** (dys-PLA-zhuh)—an abnormal structure

**frequency** (FREE-kwen-see)—how fast a sound wave moves; higher frequencies create higher-pitched sounds.

**loyal** (LOY-uhl)—having complete support for someone or something

**muscular** (MUS-kyu-lur)—having large and strong muscles

**resistant** (re-ZIS-tuhnt)—able to withstand the force or effect of something

## BOOKS

**Barnes, Nico.** *Labrador Retrievers.* Dogs. Minneapolis: Abdo Kids, 2015.

**Bowman, Chris.** *Labrador Retrievers.* Awesome Dogs. Minneapolis: Bellwether Media, 2016.

**Johnson, Jinny.** *Labrador Retriever.* My Favorite Dog. Mankato, MN: Smart Apple Media, 2013.

## WEBSITES

Labrador Retriever
**www.animalplanet.com/tv-shows/dogs-101/videos/labrador-retriever/**

The Labrador Retriever Club
**www.thelabradorclub.com**

Labrador Retriever Dog Breed Information
**www.akc.org/dog-breeds/labrador-retriever/**

# INDEX